THE INVARIABLE MARK
OF *WISDOM* IS TO
SEE THE MIRACULOUS
IN THE COMMON.

Adopt the
pace of
NATURE.
Her secret
is patience.

LOVE THE DAY.
DO NOT LEAVE
THE SKY OUT OF
YOUR LANDSCAPE.

trust t
every
vibrate
to tha
iron st

Write it

*on your **heart***

that every day

is the best day

in the year.

HAPPY
IS THE
HOUSE
THAT
SHELTERS
A
friend.

A HOME for MR. EMERSON

by **Barbara KERLEY**

illustrated by **Edwin FOTHERINGHAM**

Scholastic Press ▪ *New York*

More than anywhere else, Ralph Waldo Emerson loved his home in Concord, Massachusetts.

As a boy, he'd moved
with his family again and again as
they struggled to make ends meet.

He wandered the narrow,

noisy streets of Boston, dreaming of

*"a home, comfortable
and pleasant."*

He longed to live amid broad, open fields and deep, still woods —

in a place he could make his own.

In college, he still dreamed of fields and woods and home. But by his junior year in 1820, he also found new things to love: reading stacks of books, discussing them with friends, and recording "new thoughts" in a journal.

He named his journal *The Wide World*.

His thoughts took him everywhere.

And when he finished school and set out on his own, he wondered: *Could he build a life around these things he loved?*

In 1834, he moved to the little town of Concord, determined to find out.

He soon bought a farmhouse on the edge of a sunny meadow. He gave the house a fresh coat of white paint. Then he welcomed his new bride — Miss Lydia Jackson — who brought along her rosebushes and hens.

She sweetly called him "Mr. Emerson." He playfully called her "Queenie," or sometimes, "O Queen!" And they began their life together.

Their house would not "be fine" until trees and flowers gave it "a character of its own," Mr. Emerson knew.

"But we shall crowd so many books and papers, and, if possible, wise friends, into it that it shall have as much wit as it can carry."

Mr. Emerson and Queenie had big plans for the yard: planting fruit trees and pumpkins and corn.

They had big plans for upstairs: adding a cheerful guest wing for visitors.

But most of all, they had big plans for the study: They set up Mr. Emerson's library of books, his table, and, of course, his collection of journals, in which he wrote faithfully. Lately he'd been pondering the importance of creating the life you imagined for yourself:

"Every spirit builds itself a house,
and beyond its house a world. . . .
Build therefore your own world."

This idea and others he hoped to turn into books and lectures to support his family. Best of all, he could do this work in his peaceful study — and his nice rocking chair.

Day by day, the Emersons' house was becoming a home.

But something was missing: friends.

So Mr. Emerson sallied forth to meet the neighbors: William Munroe, who sold dry goods. Nehemiah Ball, who made boots. Phineas Allen from the Concord Academy and John Keyes at the bank. Cynthia Thoreau and Mary Brooks of the Concord Female Charitable Society, and the esteemed members of the Social Circle.

Soon, he was building friendships while also serving his community. He was appointed hog reeve, rounding up wayward hogs that strayed from their pens. He chaired the Concord School Committee and joined the volunteer fire department, his leather buckets hanging ready by the door.

Mr. Emerson helped Queenie run the household and care for their growing family — Ellen, then Edith, then Edward. And they settled into, as he put it,

"the lukewarm
milky dog days
of common
village life."

Every morning, Mr. Emerson ate pie made from his own apples for breakfast.

He led his children through the orchard,

sharing the names of the birds and varieties

of pears: Bluebird, bobolink, robin, and thrush.

Flemish Beauty, Andrews, Bartlett, and Dix.

*Then he
delved into
his collection
of books.*

In the afternoons, he walked in the woods, thinking about the books he had read and the nature that surrounded him.

He wrote down his thoughts in his journals, each one a "Savings Bank"

for his ideas.

And after he filled his journals, Mr. Emerson filled
his parlor with next-door neighbors and far-flung
friends. They spoke about literature, theology, self-reliance,
and freedom, in evenings of grand discussion.

Evenings of grand discussion gave Mr. Emerson even
more ideas to put into books and share in his lectures.
He set out for Pittsburgh, Chicago, and Troy.
Toronto, Toledo, and on to Racine. He traveled
by buggy, by steamboat, by train — to dozens of
cities for weeks at a time. . . .

And he talked.

Too many people, he observed, accepted the opinions of others instead of thinking for themselves.

"Trust thyself,"
he urged his audience.
Believe "what is true for you
in your private heart."
Believe in "the integrity
of your own mind."

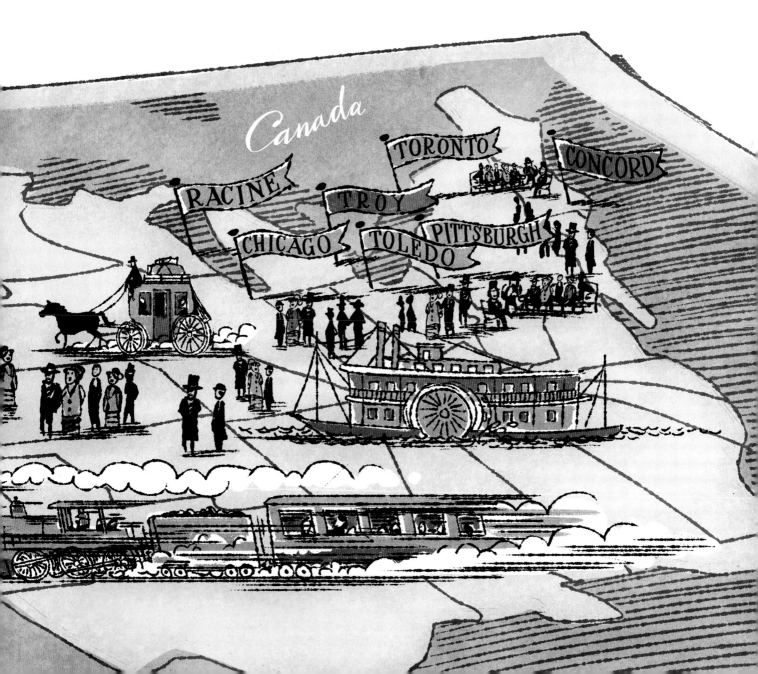

The more Mr. Emerson gave talks
and wrote books, the more people
showed up to sit in his parlor.

From nearby towns, from across the ocean, they arrived: Noblemen in glittering carriages. Poor students and famous writers. Poets. Philosophers. Kooks and cranks. Men without shoes or with beards to their waists.

But no matter how far he traveled or how famous he grew,

Mr. Emerson still loved
living in Concord.

He threw garden parties for the town's schoolchildren, with Dolly the horse

munching nearby, and Polly the parrot squawking on the stoop. He chatted

with everyone young and old on his daily walk to the post office.

The years passed. Edward moved away to study. Edith married and began a

family of her own. Ellen decided that what she wanted most of all was to care

for her mother and father — in their cozy home.

And so it was until a morning in July, 1872, when Mr. Emerson was sixty-nine years old. Ellen was away, visiting friends. Mr. Emerson and Queenie were alone.

Just before dawn, he awoke to the sound of crackling in the walls.

He got up to investigate.

A strange yellow glow seeped from a split in the plaster. Smoke poured from the hatch to the attic.

And when they opened a cupboard, flames flashed out!

Mr. Emerson ran to his front gate to summon the neighbors.

"Fire! Whitcomb!" he cried out. *"Staples! Fire!"*

Then he rushed back into the house to snatch up his papers as Queenie grabbed clothes from her closet.

Before they knew it,
the whole town
had arrived.

Arthur Gray ran through the choking smoke to gather

pictures from the walls. George Heywood threw drawers

of clothes out the bedroom window and then jumped for his life.

And one-armed Ephraim Bull Jr. clambered up to the roof with a hose.

Neighbors saved furniture, bedding, and most of Mr. Emerson's library.

But he could only wander the yard, dazed and shaken.

Such a terrible "shock to an old householder"

to see his "books and papers and stuffs and

trinkets . . . out on the grass in his door-yard."

And his home.

Oh, his home!

The Staples took in the piano, Mrs. Wetherbee, the silver, and the Whitcombs, the dining room clock. Mrs. Gregory stacked up the pictures, happy to be "returning the thousand and one favours" she'd received from the Emersons over the years.

Mr. Emerson marveled at the *"tender care"* *of his neighbors,* *but his loss* *wore heavily.*

"It is too ridiculous that a fire should make an old scholar sick," he wrote to a friend, "but the exposures of that morning, and the necessities of the following days . . . have in every way demoralized me."

Friends raised money to rebuild the house, but in his "very broken days and hours," the task seemed overwhelming.

And weeks after the fire, Mr. Emerson still felt himself an "invalid."

What Mr. Emerson needed to renew his spirit,
his friends and neighbors agreed, was to go
abroad. They urged him, as he put it,

U.S.A.

Atlantic
Ocean

"to run

across

the sea,

and

rest

and

repair."

Queenie preferred to remain
at Edith's house, but gave her
blessing for the trip.
So Mr. Emerson crossed the
Atlantic, with Ellen at his side.

Europe

Africa

In England, Mr. Emerson was relieved to have nothing that he must do. "A warm bed is the best medicine," he told Ellen. "And one gets such good sleep in this country — good strong sleep."

But he missed his gentle Queenie.

In Italy,

In Egypt, Mr. Emerson rode donkeys to pyramids and temples. He cruised hundreds of miles up the Nile on a dahabeah powered by ten oarsmen.

Then the boat swung around to begin the long . . .

slow . . .

journey back.

Day after day, the oarsmen paddled, and Mr. Emerson grew impatient —

so impatient that he and Ellen abandoned the boat for a fast train to Cairo.

Mr. Emerson was "charmed" by gardens of peppers and

palm trees and "the Mediterranean washing the picturesque shore."

But

he hungered

for letters

from

home.

He felt "very gay," he told her that evening, because he had "accomplished a good day's journey towards Concord."

"Soon, I trust," he wrote to Queenie, "we shall meet with renewed strength and unbroken faith in the heart as in the house."

Then Mr. Emerson crossed the ocean again, his face *"surely*

turned

toward

home."

Twelve days later, they were on the train to Concord:
engine huffing, wheels clacking, whistle blaring the
entire last mile, rolling into the station for one big . . .

Surprise!

"What a sight! what a sight!" Ellen later wrote a friend.

Schoolchildren raced ahead as the procession wound down the street: wagons and carriages — one even filled with babies — and Mr. Emerson in a grand barouche.

At the corner of the yard, the children reassembled. As Mr. Emerson passed under the "Welcome" arch, they began to sing

"Home,

Sweet

Home."

Home, sweet home — and sweet Queenie, waiting at the door.

Mr. Emerson fondly greeted his wife.

Then he stepped inside, amazed at all that his friends and neighbors had accomplished: The rooms were clean and bright, the furniture and knickknacks in their proper places, from the carpets on the floor to the pictures on the walls. The study was brimming with his books and papers.

Everything was cozy and inviting — just as it had been before.

Mr. Emerson went to the door and looked out at the townspeople assembled.

When he had moved to Concord so many years ago, he'd never imagined that his home would extend so far beyond the four walls of his house — to encompass the whole town. "But the fire was hardly over," he'd discovered, before "a host of friends were making the loss their own."

Now, they shared in the joy of his homecoming.

He walked down to the front gate.

"*My friends!*
I know that this is not a tribute
to an old man and his daughter
returned to their house," he said,
but rather a tribute to
"*us all — one family — in Concord!*"

The crowd gave three hearty cheers!

Mr. Emerson
was home.

AUTHOR'S NOTE

Emerson (top center) and Queenie (to his left) in front of their Concord home with their children and grandchildren, 1879.

It's no surprise that Ralph Waldo Emerson loved inviting people to his home in Concord. It was a vibrant community of neighbors and friends, fellow thinkers and writers — and they were all drawn to Emerson.

Henry David Thoreau, author of *Walden*, built a cabin on land Emerson owned by Walden Pond and then lived there for over two years. Nathaniel Hawthorne, author of *The Scarlet Letter*, took Emerson ice skating and ate strawberries and cream at his house. And Louisa May Alcott, author of *Little Women*, spent her childhood borrowing books from Emerson's study. In later years, she called him "my Ralph."

Emerson appreciated the wealth of ideas his friends and neighbors in Concord brought into his parlor. And he drew strength from their friendship.

He'd arrived in 1834, still grieving the loss of his first wife, Ellen Louisa Tucker, who had died of tuberculosis in 1831, just sixteen months after their marriage. His Concord community offered support and comfort again in 1842, when Emerson and Lydia — his second wife — lost their first child, Waldo, to scarlet fever at age five.

As Emerson's fame and influence grew, he would have been welcomed with open arms in communities around the country and abroad. Yet he remained in Concord for the rest of his life, for nestled in this creative, supportive environment, he did his best work.

Writing at a time when America was emerging as a new country and forging its own identity, Emerson declared, "We have listened too long to the courtly muses of Europe." It was time, instead, to "speak our own minds."

Through his books, lectures, even the conversations in his parlor, Emerson encouraged people to "look at the world with new eyes." More than any other writer, his ideas about self-reliance, independence, and the unlimited potential of every individual have come to define the American spirit.

Emerson has been gone for more than a century, and yet his influence lives on. His gravesite remains a place where people visit, leaving pens and pencils, acorns, coins, and pebbles behind — small tokens of appreciation for a man who continues to inspire writers, challenge readers, and change lives.

BUILD A WORLD OF YOUR OWN

Mr. Emerson built his world around the things he loved. You can do this, too — because *you* get to choose the life you create for yourself. Use the ideas below to help you get started. Just like Mr. Emerson, be sure to record your thoughts in a notebook or journal.

"The great business of life is to learn ourselves."

Before you can build your world, you must know yourself. Mr. Emerson was a thinker and a reader who loved writing in his journal, walking in nature, and spending time with family and friends at home. What type of person are you?

- Choose five words that best describe you.
- List five things you love to do.

Mr. Emerson created a job out of his love of reading, thinking, and exploring ideas. What kind of job would you enjoy?

- List your three favorite subjects in school.
- List three other things you'd like to learn more about.
- List jobs people around you do. Add to this list other jobs that sound interesting. Circle the jobs that seem the most fun.

"Happy is the house that shelters a friend!"

Mr. Emerson wanted a home with a quiet study, a parlor for visitors, and an orchard and garden. What kind of home do you want?

- Think about your favorite room. What do you like about it?
- Design your perfect home. What rooms would you include? What would the outdoor space look like?

From a young age, Mr. Emerson knew he wanted to live surrounded by nature. Where might you want to live one day?

- Get to know your city or town by exploring. Write down your five favorite spots.
- Add to this any favorite places you've visited on trips. You can even visit Mr. Emerson's home — a National Historic Landmark — from April through October. Ralph Waldo Emerson Memorial House, 28 Cambridge Turnpike, Concord, Massachusetts.
- Look at your list and determine what kinds of places you like best. Create a map of your perfect place to live.

"Make yourself necessary to somebody."

Mr. Emerson loved people and wanted to be active in his community, so he did volunteer work and threw garden parties for the neighborhood children. Your community includes neighbors, friends, classmates and teachers, teammates and coaches, and people in the clubs you join. How would you like to be part of your community?

- List your three favorite community activities. Why do you like them?
- Experiment and take action! Broaden your experiences by joining a new club, volunteering with an organization, or finding a way to help your neighbors. Then write about this experience in your journal.

Keep your journal in a safe place. Like Mr. Emerson, you can add "new thoughts" as you grow — meeting new people, visiting new places, and trying new activities. Soon, you'll be well on your way to building a world around the things you love!

"Every spirit builds itself a house, and beyond its house a world. . . .
Build therefore your own world."

For Amy and Courtney, who always make me feel at home — B.K.

For my family, and for Tracy Mack and Marijka Kostiw: Thanks for pushing! — E.F.

ACKNOWLEDGMENTS

The author and illustrator gratefully acknowledge Ronald A. Bosco, Vincent O'Leary Professor of English and American Literature, University at Albany, SUNY, for fact-checking the book; Marie Gordinier and Christine Brown of the Ralph Waldo Emerson Memorial House, Concord, MA; Leslie Perrin Wilson of the Concord Free Public Library; the Concord Museum; Multnomah County Library, Oregon; the Portland State University Branford P. Millar Library, Oregon; and the Houghton Library, Harvard College Library, Harvard University.

QUOTATIONS IN THE TEXT ARE DRAWN FROM THE FOLLOWING SOURCES:

"a home, comfortable . . .": Ralph L. Rusk, ed., *The Letters of Ralph Waldo Emerson* (New York: Columbia University Press, 1939), 1:57.

"new thoughts" and "The Wide World": William H. Gilman, Alfred R. Ferguson, George P. Clark, and Merrell R. Davis, eds., *The Journals and Miscellaneous Notebooks of Ralph Waldo Emerson* (Cambridge, MA: Belknap Press of Harvard University Press, 1960), 1:3.

"Mr. Emerson": Gay Wilson Allen, *Waldo Emerson* (New York: The Viking Press, 1981), 244.

"Queenie": William H. Gilman, Alfred R. Ferguson, et al, *Journals*, 8:242.

"O Queen!": Delores Bird Carpenter, ed., Ellen Tucker Emerson, *The Life of Lidian Jackson Emerson* (Boston: Twayne Publishers, 1980), 92.

"be fine", "a character . . .", and, "But we shall . . .": Rusk, *Letters*, 1:447.

"Every spirit . . .": Brooks Atkinson, ed., "Nature," *The Essential Writings of Ralph Waldo Emerson* (New York: The Modern Library, 2000), 39.

"the lukewarm . . .": William H. Gilman, Alfred R. Ferguson, Harrison Hayford, and Merton M. Sealts, eds., *Journals*, 5:420.

"Savings Bank": William H. Gilman, Alfred R. Ferguson, Merrell R. Davis, Harrison Hayford, and Merton M. Sealts, eds., *Journals*, 4:250.

"Trust thyself", "what is true . . .", and, "the integrity . . .": Atkinson, "Self-Reliance," *Essential Writings*, 132-135.

"Fire! Whitcomb! . . .": Edith E. W. Gregg, ed., *The Letters of Ellen Tucker Emerson* (Ohio: The Kent State University Press, 1982), 1:678.

"shock to an . . ." and "books and papers . . .": Rusk, *Letters*, 6:219.

"returning the . . .": Gregg, *Letters of Ellen Tucker Emerson*, 1:680.

"tender care": Eleanor M. Tilton, ed., *The Letters of Ralph Waldo Emerson* (New York: Columbia University Press, 1995), 10:85.

"It is too ridiculous . . .": Tilton, *Letters*, 10:86.

"very broken . . .": Tilton, *Letters*, 10:93.

"invalid": Tilton, *Letters*, 10:88.

"to run across . . .": Rusk, *Letters*, 6:219.

"A warm bed . . ." and "And one gets . . .": Gregg, *Letters of Ellen Tucker Emerson*, 2:57.

"charmed" and "the Mediterranean. . .": Rusk, *Letters*, 6:228.

"very gay" and "accomplished a good. . .": Gregg, *Letters of Ellen Tucker Emerson*, 2:57.

"Soon, I trust. . .": Rusk, *Letters*, 6:234.

"surely turned. . .": Tilton, *Letters*, 10:109.

"What a sight. . .": Gregg, *Letters of Ellen Tucker Emerson*, 2:90.

"But the fire. . ." and "a host of. . .": Tilton, *Letters*, 10:98.

"My friends. . ." and "us all. . .": Edward Waldo Emerson, *Emerson In Concord* (Detroit: Gale Research Company, 1970), 187.

QUOTATIONS IN THE AUTHOR'S NOTE ARE DRAWN FROM THE FOLLOWING SOURCES:

"my Ralph": Ronald A. Bosco and Joel Myerson, eds., *Emerson In His Own Time* (Iowa City: University of Iowa Press, 2003), 64.

"We have listened. . ." and "speak our own minds": Atkinson, "The American Scholar," *Essential Writings*, 59.

"look at the world. . .": Atkinson, "Nature," *Essential Writings*, 39.

"The great business . . .": William H. Gilman, Alfred R. Ferguson, Merrell R. Davis, Harrison Hayford, and Merton M. Sealts, eds., *Journals*, 3:144

"Happy is the. . .": Atkinson, "Friendship," *Essential Writings*, 206.

"Make yourself. . .": E.W. Emerson, "Considerations By The Way," *The Complete Works of Ralph Waldo Emerson*. Concord Edition. (Boston: Houghton Mifflin, 1904), 6:275.

"Every spirit. . .": Atkinson, "Nature," *Essential Writings*, 39.

"'Tis the good . . .": E.W. Emerson, "Success," *Complete Works*, concord Edition, 7:296

QUOTATIONS ON THE BOOK JACKET AND ENDPAPERS ARE DRAWN FROM THE FOLLOWING SOURCES:

"Adopt the pace . . .": E. W. Emerson, "Education," *Complete Works*, Concord Edition, 10:155.

"All life is . . .": Edward Waldo Emerson and Waldo Emerson Forbes, eds., *The Journals of Ralph Waldo Emerson* (Boston and New York: Houghton Mifflin, 1909-1914), 6:299.

"Insist on yourself . . .": Atkinson, "Self-Reliance," *The Essential Writings*, 150.

"It is a . . .": William H. Gilman, Alfred R. Ferguson, Harrison Hayford, and Merton M. Sealts, eds., *Journals*, 5:32.

"Love the day . . ." and "Scatter joy . . .": E.W. Emerson, "Behavior," *Complete Works*, Concord Edition, 6:196.

"Nothing great was . . .": Atkinson, "Circles," *Essential Writings*, 262.

"The invariable . . .": Atkinson, "Nature," *Essential Writings*, 38.

"The only way . . .": Atkinson, "Friendship," *Essential Writings*, 211.

"There is then . . .": Atkinson, "The American Scholar," *Essential Writings*, 48.

"Trust thyself . . .": Atkinson, "Self-Reliance," *Essential Writings*, 133.

"Write it . . .": E.W. Emerson, "Works And Days," *Complete Works*, Concord Edition, 7:175.

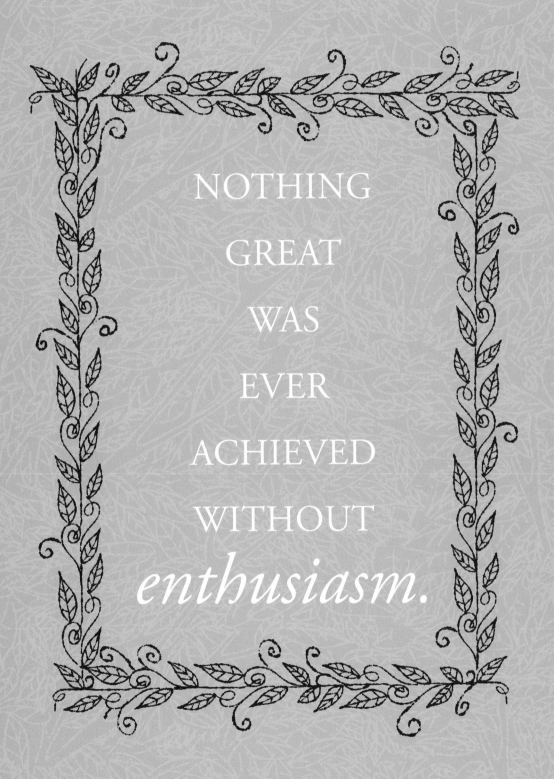

NOTHING
GREAT
WAS
EVER
ACHIEVED
WITHOUT
enthusiasm.

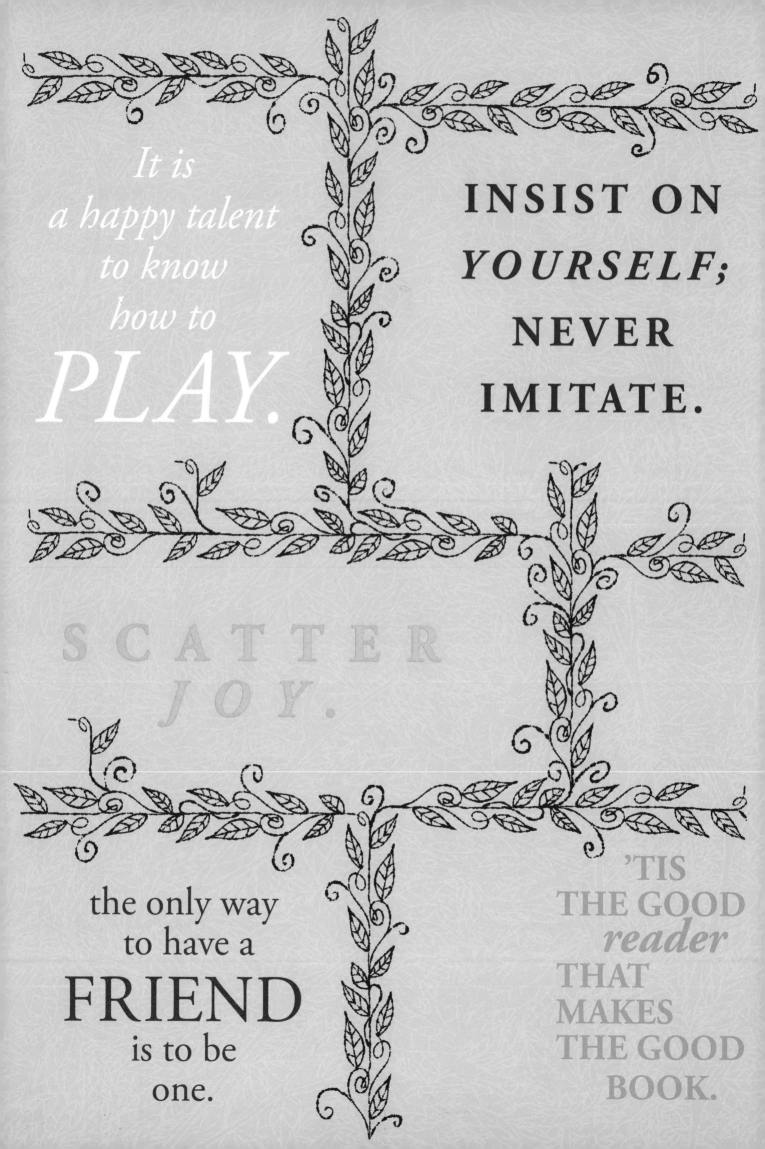

It is a happy talent to know how to **PLAY.**

INSIST ON YOURSELF; NEVER IMITATE.

SCATTER JOY.

the only way to have a **FRIEND** is to be one.

'TIS THE GOOD *reader* THAT MAKES THE GOOD BOOK.